MW01154463

KENTUCKY

by Patricia Lantier

GARETH**STEVENS**
PUBLISHING
A Member of the WRC Media Family of Companies

Please visit our web site at: www.garethstevens.com
For a free color catalog describing Gareth Stevens Publishing's
list of high-quality books and multimedia programs, call
1-800-542-2595 (USA) or 1-800-387-3178 (Canada).
Gareth Stevens Publishing's fax: (414) 332-3567.

Library of Congress Cataloging-in-Publication Data

Lantier, Patricia, 1952-
  Kentucky / Patricia Lantier.
    p. cm. — (Portraits of the states)
  Includes bibliographical references and index.
  ISBN 0-8368-4666-4 (lib. bdg.)
  ISBN 0-8368-4685-0 (softcover)
  1. Kentucky—Juvenile literature. I. Title. II. Series.
F451.3.L36   2006
76.9—dc22   2005044476

This edition first published in 2006 by
Gareth Stevens Publishing
A Member of the WRC Media Family of Companies
330 West Olive Street, Suite 100
Milwaukee, WI 53212 USA

This edition copyright © 2006 by Gareth Stevens, Inc.

Editorial direction: Mark J. Sachner
Project manager: Jonatha A. Brown
Editor: Catherine Gardner
Art direction and design: Tammy West
Picture research: Diane Laska-Swanke
Indexer: Walter Kronenberg
Production: Jessica Morris and Robert Kraus

Picture credits: Cover, pp. 15, 18, 21, 24, 25, 27, 29 © www.adamjonesphoto.com;
p. 4 © PhotoDisc; p. 5 © Corel; pp. 6, 28 © Library of Congress; p. 8 © MPI/
Hulton Archive/Getty Images; pp. 9, 17 © Hulton Archive/Getty Images; p. 11
© Francis Miller/Time & Life Pictures/Getty Images; p. 12 Kentucky Department
of Libraries and Archives; p. 16 © Don Cravens/Time & Life Pictures/Getty
Images; p. 22 Toyota Motor Manufacturing, Kentucky, Inc.; p. 26 © Gibson
Stock Photography

Printed in the United States of America

1 2 3 4 5 6 7 8 9 10 09 08 07 06

CONTENTS

Words that are defined in the Glossary appear
in **bold** the first time they are used in the text.

On the Cover: Calumet Farm is a famous horse breeding and racing
farm. It is located near Lexington.

Introduction

If you could visit Kentucky, what would you like to see? The dark Mammoth Cave? A **bluegrass** music concert? The Kentucky Derby horse race?

Kentucky is a great place to visit. This state has forests, mountains and white-water rivers. It has coalfields and **plains**. It also has special music and some of the fastest horses in the world.

The people of Kentucky work hard. They like to rely on their own resources. They also enjoy showing visitors the many wonders of their beautiful state.

Welcome to Kentucky!

This horse farm is in the Bluegrass Region of Kentucky. The home at the end of the drive was once a plantation.

The state flag of Kentucky.

KENTUCKY FACTS

- Became the 15th U.S. State: June 1, 1792
- Population (2004): 4,145,922
- Capital: Frankfort
- Biggest Cities: Lexington, Louisville, Owensboro, Bowling Green
- Size: 39,728 square miles (102,895 square kilometers)
- Nickname: The Bluegrass State
- State Tree: Tulip tree
- State Flower: Goldenrod
- State Wild Animal: Gray squirrel
- State Bird: Cardinal

History

People have lived in the Kentucky area for thousands of years. The earliest groups lived by hunting large animals. Later Native Americans began to farm. One tribe, the Adena, was also called Mound Builders. The Adena lived in the region and built large mounds of earth or stone to bury their dead.

Other groups also settled in the area. But by the time the first white settlers arrived, not many Natives still lived there. No one is sure why these people moved away from the area.

Explorers, Settlers, and Statehood

Early settlers had a hard time getting to Kentucky. They had no easy way to cross the mountains. Also, the Natives who

Daniel Boone was a famous frontiersman. He helped settlers reach the Kentucky area by leading them through the Cumberland Gap.

American Pioneer

Daniel Boone was a hunter, trapper, and explorer. He explored the American frontier. He made many trips into the Kentucky wilderness. He even moved his own family there. In 1775, a trading company hired Boone to make a trail for new settlers to move into Kentucky. It was called the Wilderness Road. Because of Boone's skill and hard work, many people settled in the area.

lived there did not want the settlers to move in. Daniel Boone made many trips to Kentucky. He explored the area and came to know it well. He helped open the Wilderness Road for new settlers to travel. This road brought them through the Cumberland Gap, a pass through the mountains.

The first white settlement in the Kentucky region was Fort Harrod. It was founded on June 16, 1774. It is now called Harrodsburg. Daniel Boone also helped start a settlement in the Kentucky lands. It was called Fort Boonesborough. The land for the fort was bought from the Cherokee people.

The land was bought from the Cherokee before the American Revolution. After the war, the state of Virginia said the land purchase was not legal. It took control of most of the Kentucky land. More settlers moved to Kentucky. The people began to hold special meetings. They wanted to form their own state. On June 1, 1792, the Commonwealth of Kentucky joined the nation as the fifteenth U.S. state.

Kentucky began to grow in the early 1800s. People built **canals** and railroads to

FUN FACTS

For the People

Kentucky is a commonwealth as well as a state. This means the state has laws that are based on the **consent** of the people who live there. The people have agreed that the state laws are for the common good of all.

IN KENTUCKY'S HISTORY

Costly Conflict

Soldiers from the North and South fought in Perryville in 1862. It was one of the worst battles fought in Kentucky. Union forces won the battle. More than seven thousand soldiers were killed or injured.

link towns and cities in the state. Farmers could sell their crops in many places. During this time, the most important crops were **hemp**, tobacco, and grains.

A State Divided

Slavery was legal in Kentucky. Farmers who owned a lot of land often had slaves. Small farmers who did not have slaves did not want the slave system. It helped big farmers who had slaves make much more money. Other people did not want slavery because they believed it was wrong.

Many farmers in Kentucky had slaves before the Civil War. After the war, former slaves could hardly make a living. This photo is from 1870.

Civil War

The people of Kentucky could not agree whether to break away, or **secede**, from the Union before the Civil War began. So the state remained **neutral**. It did not choose a side. People in the state, both black and white, fought in the war anyway. Some people fought for the North, or the Union. Others joined the South, or the Confederate States of America. Many battles were fought in Kentucky. After four years, the Union won the war.

FUN FACTS

Native Name

Most people agree that the name *Kentucky* comes from a Native American word. But not everyone agrees on what the word is. The most likely choice is *ken-tah-ten*. It is an Iroquoian word that means "land of tomorrow."

Famous People of Kentucky

Jefferson Davis

Born: June 3, 1808, Davisburg (now Fairview), Kentucky

Died: December 6, 1889, New Orleans, Louisiana

Jefferson Davis was born in Kentucky. He was the youngest of ten children. When he was young, his family moved to another state. Later, he went to college in Kentucky. Davis was a respected **statesman**. He is known mainly as the president of the Confederate States of America during the Civil War.

Recovery

After the war, the U.S. government sent soldiers to the Southern states. They helped restore order to the area. They also made sure that former slaves had equal rights. People in the state felt the soldiers should not be there. Their state had not taken sides in the Civil War.

The people of Kentucky had a hard time after the war. The only large city in the state was Louisville. Farming was still the main way of earning a living. More railroads and new roads were needed to help the **economy**. But it took a while for roads and railroads to be built.

Close to the end of the nineteenth century, coal mining became important in the state. New railroads helped move the coal to many places. People who owned the mines made a lot of money. The miners did not. They began to form groups called **unions**. The unions helped miners get fair pay and better working conditions.

A New Century

World War I and World War II were fought in the first half of the twentieth century.

IN KENTUCKY'S HISTORY

Family Feuds

In the late 1800s, some mountain families began to feud, or fight with each other. Sometimes, they fought because they had been on different sides in the Civil War. One of the most famous feuds was the one between the Hatfield and McCoy families. It began when the McCoys said the Hatfields had stolen one of their hogs. This feud lasted about ten years. At least ten men died.

Both wars took place overseas. Soldiers from Kentucky and all the other states fought in these two wars.

During World War I, coal production in the state grew. This helped the economy for a while. But the **Great Depression** began in the early 1930s. During this time, the prices people paid for goods fell. Workers everywhere lost their jobs. Kentucky had a hard time, too. A program called the New Deal helped. President Franklin D. Roosevelt gave the people work to do in the state. The people built roads and schools. They also built dams over some rivers to stop flooding.

IN KENTUCKY'S HISTORY

A Coal Miner's Life
Early mine owners did not treat their workers well. They owned the houses the miners lived in. They forced the miners to buy food from stores the mines owned. They did not even pay the miners in dollars. Instead, they paid them in scrip. This was a type of "money" the mine owners made up. The mine owners controlled the people who worked for them.

In the twentieth century, Kentucky mined huge amounts of coal. These men are working at a small coal mine.

Georgia Powers (center) helped African Americans get the same rights as white people. She is shown here with baseball great Jackie Robinson (left) and Dr. Martin Luther King Jr.

After World War II, the people in the state began to work on equal rights for all people. Slavery had ended with the Civil War. But this did not mean all people were treated fairly. The Kentucky Civil Rights Act was passed in 1966. This law promised equal rights to all of the citizens. A woman named

Georgia Powers became a leader in the state's Civil Rights movement. In 1967, she became the first African American and the first woman ever elected to the State Senate.

Today in Kentucky

The state still mines a lot of coal. Many people now have jobs in service, technology, and manufacturing fields. Georgetown has a huge Toyota automobile plant. It hopes to start making a new energy-saving hybrid Camry line in 2006.

★ ★ ★ Time Line ★ ★ ★

c. 1000 B.C.	Adena Mound Builders in Kentucky make huge mounds to bury their dead.
1775	A trading company hires frontiersman Daniel Boone to blaze a trail for new settlers going to Kentucky. This new trail becomes known as the Wilderness Road.
1792	Kentucky becomes the fifteenth U.S. state. It is called the Commonwealth of Kentucky.
1861–1865	The North fights the South in the Civil War. In 1862, the fierce Battle of Perryville is fought in Kentucky. Thousands of men are either injured or killed in the battle.
1917–1918	Soldiers from Kentucky fight alongside other U.S. troops in World War I.
1930s	The Great Depression causes hardship in Kentucky and all other U.S. states. The coal mining industry helps provide jobs for some.
1941–1945	Kentucky sends soldiers to fight in World War II.
1966	The Kentucky Civil Rights Act is passed.
1967	Georgia Powers, a leader in the Kentucky Civil Rights movement, is the first African American and the first woman elected to the State Senate.
1999	Kentucky Virtual University is launched. It has become a model for adult education and long-distance learning in the country.
2006	The Toyota automobile manufacturing plant in Georgetown hopes to begin production of a new gasoline-electric hybrid Camry line.

13

People

Kentucky has more than four million people. A little more than half of the people in the state live in small towns and cities. Lexington and Louisville are the only large cities. Slightly less than half of the people in the state live in **rural** areas.

Native Americans have lived on this land for at least fourteen thousand years. The Native **population** today is not very large. They number about 8,500 people.

Hispanics: In the 2000 U.S. Census, 1.5 percent of the people in Kentucky called themselves Latino or Hispanic. Most of them or their relatives came from places where Spanish is spoken. They may come from different racial backgrounds.

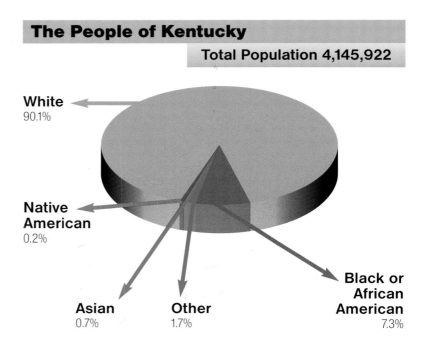

The People of Kentucky

Total Population 4,145,922

White
90.1%

Native
American
0.2%

Asian
0.7%

Other
1.7%

Black or
African
American
7.3%

Percentages are based on the 2000 Census.

The first settlers came mainly from Britain and Germany. Today, more than ninety percent of the people who live in the state are white.

At the time of the Civil War, about one-fourth of the people were black. Most were slaves. After the war, many moved to northern states. They hoped for a better life in their new homes. Today, African

The city of Louisville is located on the Ohio River. It was founded in 1778 by George Rogers Clark and was named after King Louis XVI of France.

Americans make up about 7 percent of the population.

Education

The state had a few public schools before the Civil War. But the school system broke down after the war. By the early 1900s, many people in

In 1956, children of all races started attending the same schools in Kentucky. Sometimes, National Guardsmen made sure there was no trouble.

the state could not read or write. The Sullivan Law was passed in 1908. This law created a new school system for the state.

The new school system raised the money it needed through county taxes. Some counties had more money than others. The schools with more money often were better than the schools with little money. In 1990, the General Assembly passed the Kentucky Reform Act. The districts now try to make sure that all schools in the state have more equal funds.

Today, Kentucky has many strong colleges and universities. Some of them are public, and some of them are private. The Kentucky Virtual University went online in 1999. It is a model for the future. Students who cannot attend regular classes can study and earn degrees at home.

Religion

About 90 percent of the people in Kentucky are Christians. Almost half of the Christians are Baptists. Close to 13 percent are Catholics. About 7 percent are Methodists. Some Jews, Buddhists, and Muslims live in the state, too.

Carry Nation worked to stop the use of alcohol and tobacco. She also worked for women's rights.

Famous People of Kentucky

Carry Nation

Born: November 25, 1846, Garrard County, Kentucky

Died: June 9, 1911, Leavenworth, Kansas

Carry Nation did not believe people should drink alcohol. She spent her adult life fighting for this cause. In 1880, Kansas passed a law that said alcohol could not be made or sold except for use as medicine. Carry Nation decided to help enforce this law. She joined the Women's Christian Temperance Union. This group worked to stop the sale and use of alcohol. Carry Nation used bricks, hatchets, and hammers to destroy places that sold alcohol. She did everything she could to help enforce the law.

The Land

Kentucky has five main regions. The land farthest west is the Jackson Purchase. It is named after Andrew Jackson, the seventh president of the United States. Jackson had helped buy the land from the Chickasaw tribe in 1818. The region has low hills and valleys. It has good land for farming.

North and east of the Jackson Purchase is the Western Coal Field. This region is hilly. It also has rich farmland.

The Pennyroyal Region lies east, west, and south of the Western Coal

The Kentucky River Palisades is in the Bluegrass Region. It is a planned area that protects rare, native plants and animals.

KENTUCKY

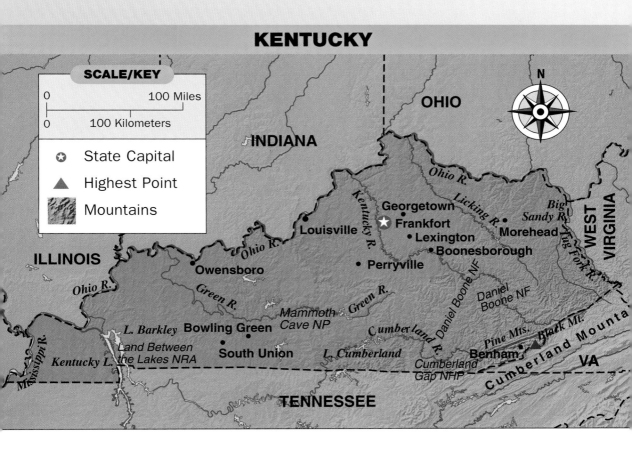

SCALE/KEY

0 — 100 Miles
0 — 100 Kilometers

⊛ State Capital
▲ Highest Point
Mountains

OHIO

INDIANA

ILLINOIS

Ohio R.

Licking R.

Georgetown
⊛ Frankfort
Louisville
Lexington
Morehead
Boonesborough

Kentucky R.

Big Sandy R.

WEST VIRGINIA

Tug Fork R.

Owensboro

Perryville

Green R.

Green R.

Mammoth
Cave NP

Daniel Boone NF

Daniel
Boone NF

Cumberland R.

Pine Mts.

Black Mt.

Cumberland Mounta

L. Barkley
Bowling Green
Land Between
the Lakes NRA
South Union
L. Cumberland
Benham
VA

Kentucky L.

Cumberland
Gap NHP

Mississippi R.

TENNESSEE

Field. It is named for a type
of mint plant that grows
there. This area has some
hills called knobs. It also
has sandstone cliffs and
limestone. Many caves are
in this part of the state.

The Bluegrass Region is
next. The oldest rocks in
the state lie under the soil
there. The soil is rich in
limestone. The land is good
for crops and has grass for
grazing animals. This area
has beautiful farmland and
rolling hills. Many of the
state's famous horse farms
are in this region.

In the eastern part of the
state is the Eastern Coal
Field Region. It is mountain
country. The soil has lots of

sand and clay. Kentucky's highest point, called Black Mountain, is in this region. It is near the state's eastern border. It stands 4,145 feet (1,264 meters) high.

Climate

Kentucky has a mild climate. Summers are warm and can

Major Rivers	
Mississippi River 2,357 miles (3,792 km) long	
Ohio River 975 miles (1,569 km) long	
Cumberland River 687 miles (1,105 km) long	

sometimes get hot. Winters are cool. About 50 inches (1,270 millimeters) of rain fall in the state each year. Several inches of snow can fall in the mountainous areas. Tornadoes often are a problem in the state.

Waterways

The state has several rivers, including the Mississippi, Ohio, Cumberland, and Kentucky Rivers. Other main rivers are the Big Sandy and the Tug Fork. The state does not have many natural lakes. Most of the lakes are man-made. They have been

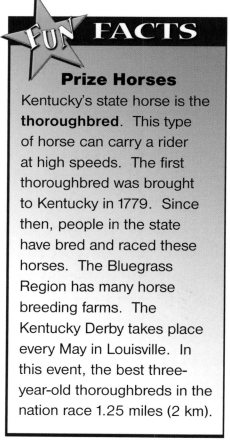

FUN FACTS

Prize Horses

Kentucky's state horse is the **thoroughbred**. This type of horse can carry a rider at high speeds. The first thoroughbred was brought to Kentucky in 1779. Since then, people in the state have bred and raced these horses. The Bluegrass Region has many horse breeding farms. The Kentucky Derby takes place every May in Louisville. In this event, the best three-year-old thoroughbreds in the nation race 1.25 miles (2 km).

created by building dams across the rivers. Kentucky Lake is the largest in the state. It is a man-made lake.

Plants and Animals

Nearly half of the state is forest. Daniel Boone National Forest covers a great part of the southeast. Beech, hickory, sugar maple, and oak are some of the types of trees that grow in the state. The flowering tulip is the state tree. It can grow up to 190 feet (58 m) high. Wildflowers and shrubs, such as violets, asters, and dogwoods, also grow freely. Goldenrod is the state flower.

Snow geese, wood ducks, and great blue herons are a few of the many birds that live in Kentucky. The state bird is the cardinal. More than two hundred types of fish, such as catfish, bass, and bluegill, live in the state's waterways.

Black bears, foxes, and red wolves are a few of the wild animals in Kentucky. The state wild animal is the gray squirrel.

The Cumberland River is a great place to hike, camp, and enjoy water sports. This river has a 68-foot (20-m) waterfall.

Economy

Most early settlers in Kentucky were farmers. This started to change in the late 1800s. People began to build **factories** and make goods to sell. The state had plenty of coal for power.

Making automobiles is big business in the state now. About 10 percent of all the cars and trucks in the country today are made in Kentucky.

Farming and Mining

Not as many people farm today. But the state still has many small farms. The

Toyota Motor Manufacturing is in Georgetown. The plant has produced more than six million vehicles since 1986. This vehicle is moving through the assembly line.

main crop is tobacco. Some people raise beef cattle and dairy cows. Thoroughbred horses are the state's most famous livestock.

Coal mining is important to the state. Workers often use strip mining to reach the coal. In this kind of mining, the top layer of soil is taken off to reach the coal below. Strip mining destroys the soil and pollutes the water. Companies that do strip mining must restore the land after they have taken out all of the coal.

Tourism

Tourism is growing in the state. Visitors want to see the beautiful scenery. They also travel here to enjoy the music, crafts, and history. Thousands of people go to the Kentucky Derby each year. All of these visitors bring a lot of money to the state.

How Money Is Made in Kentucky

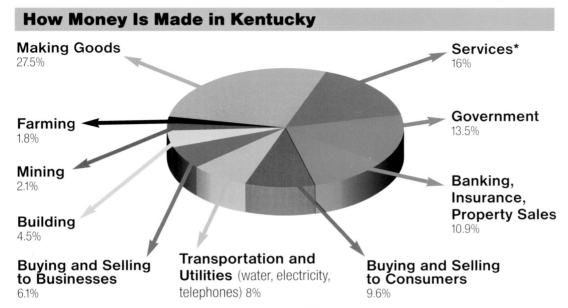

Making Goods
27.5%

Services*
16%

Farming
1.8%

Government
13.5%

Mining
2.1%

Building
4.5%

Banking, Insurance, Property Sales
10.9%

Buying and Selling to Businesses
6.1%

Transportation and Utilities (water, electricity, telephones) 8%

Buying and Selling to Consumers
9.6%

* Services include jobs in hotels, restaurants, auto repair, medicine, teaching, and entertainment.

23

CHAPTER 6

Government

rankfort is Kentucky's capital city. The state's lawmakers work there. The government has three parts, or branches. The parts are the executive, legislative, and judicial branches.

Executive Branch

The governor is head of the executive branch. This branch makes sure all of the state laws are carried out. The lieutenant governor helps the governor. Other officials also belong to the executive branch.

Legislative Branch

The legislative branch makes state laws.

Kentucky's State Capitol in Frankfort was built in 1910. It is the state's fourth capitol since it joined the Union in 1792.

The legislature, called the General Assembly, has two parts. They are the Senate and the House of Representatives. The two parts work together.

The Kentucky governor's mansion was built in 1914. It is open to the public for tours.

Judicial Branch

Judges and courts make up the judicial branch. When a person is accused of a crime, the judges and courts may decide whether that person is guilty.

Local Government

Kentucky has 120 counties. Each county is led by a team of officials who are elected. The team is called the fiscal court. It takes care of the county's business. The head of the fiscal court is the county judge.

KENTUCKY'S STATE GOVERNMENT

Executive		Legislative		Judicial	
Office	**Length of Term**	**Body**	**Length of Term**	**Court**	**Length of Term**
Governor	4 years	Senate (38 members)	4 years	Supreme (7 justices)	8 years
Lieutenant Governor	4 years	House of Representatives (100 members)	2 years	Appeals (14 judges)	8 years

Mammoth Cave National Park has the largest system of caves and underground tunnels in the world.

Things to See and Do

The people of Kentucky want tourists to see their state. There are many fun things to do and places to visit. The state has something for everyone.

Plenty of Parks

Kentucky has lots of parks. Cumberland State Resort Park is special. When the moon is full, mist from the park's waterfall creates a "moonbow." This is a rainbow created by moonlight. Mammoth Cave National Park has hiking trails. It also has places to canoe and fish on the Green River. Underground, it has the longest known cave system in the world.

Museums and Historic Sites

Museums celebrate the state's history. Morehead

State University is home to the Kentucky Folk Art Center. It shows the work of local folk and craft artists.

The Kentucky Military History Center is located in Frankfort. The state also shows special honor to those who fought in the Civil War. It has marked the location of more than fifty battles in Kentucky along the Civil War Discovery Trail.

The Kentucky Coal Mining Museum is in Benham. This collection has old train cars that once carried miners to their underground jobs. It also has mining tools and a piece of coal that weighs two tons!

New Music

Bluegrass music began in Kentucky. This type of

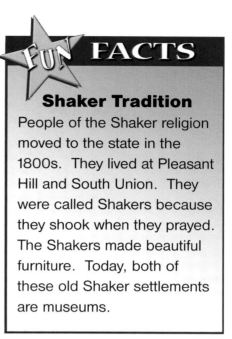

Shaker Tradition

People of the Shaker religion moved to the state in the 1800s. They lived at Pleasant Hill and South Union. They were called Shakers because they shook when they prayed. The Shakers made beautiful furniture. Today, both of these old Shaker settlements are museums.

This spiral stairway is part of the Trustee House at the Shaker Village of Pleasant Hill.

Famous People of Kentucky

Abraham Lincoln

Born: February 12, 1809, Hodgenville, Kentucky

Died: April 15, 1865, Washington, D.C.

Abe Lincoln was born in a log cabin. He did not attend school for long. But he studied on his own and became a lawyer. In 1860, he was elected the sixteenth U.S. president. The Civil War began soon after

he took office. Lincoln wanted the states to stay together. He also wanted to end slavery. After four years, the Union won the war. A few days after the war ended, an actor named John Wilkes Booth shot Lincoln at a theater. He died the next day. He was one of the country's most beloved presidents.

country music was created by a band called Bill Monroe and the Blue Grass Boys. The music is named after the band. Usually, five people play in a bluegrass band. A bluegrass band most often includes string instruments.

Sports

The most famous sports event in the state may be the Kentucky Derby. It is called the "Run for the Roses." Thoroughbred horses have raced in the Derby every year in May since 1875. The race is in Louisville.

Famous People of Kentucky

Loretta Lynn

Born: April 14, 1935, Butcher Hollow, Kentucky

Loretta Webb Lynn is a famous country music singer. She was the daughter of a coal miner. As a child, she sang at church. She married Oliver Lynn at age thirteen. As Lynn became a star, she sang songs that told women to be strong and take charge of their lives. A movie about her life was made in 1980. It was titled *Coal Miner's Daughter*. Lynn has recorded seventy music albums. She has won many awards.

Kentucky does not have major league sports teams. But its college teams have lots of fans. This is especially true for the University of Kentucky in Lexington and the University of Louisville. Both of these universities usually have strong basketball teams.

The Kentucky Derby is perhaps the most famous horse race in the country. The fastest three-year-old thoroughbred horses race each year at Churchill Downs track in Louisville.

bluegrass — a type of music started in Kentucky. It also is a type of grass that is green with bluish stems and tips.

canals — channels dug across land that connect bodies of water so ships can go between them

consent — approval

economy — the system of using money and resources in an organization or state

factories — buildings where goods and products are made

Great Depression — a time, in the 1930s, when many people lost jobs and and businesses lost money

hemp — a type of herb that has tough fibers and often is used to make rope

limestone — a type of rock that is formed mainly by once-living material, such as coral or shells

neutral — not taking sides

plains — large areas of flat land

population — the number of people who live in a place, such as a state

rural — something that is in the country

secede — to formally quit or get out of a group

statesman — a person who is a leader in the government

thoroughbred — a type of racehorse that is bred for lightness and speed, or an animal that is a pure breed

unions — groups of people united for a cause

Books

B Is for Bluegrass: A Kentucky Alphabet. Discover America State by State (series). Mary Ann McCabe Riehle (Sleeping Bear Press)

The Boy Who Drew Birds: A Story of John James Audubon. Jacqueline Davies (Houghton Mifflin)

Daniel Boone. On My Own Biographies (series). Tom Streissguth (Lerner)

Down Cut Shin Creek: The Pack Horse Librarians of Kentucky. Kathi Appelt (HarperCollins)

Kentucky. Rookie Read-About Geography (series). Kim Valzania (Children's Press)

A Personal Tour of a Shaker Village. How It Was (series). Michael Capek (Lerner)

Web Sites

Abraham Lincoln Birthplace (National Historic Site)
www.nps.gov/abli/linchomj.htm

Kentucky: Bluegrass State
www.kidskonnect.com/Kentucky/KentuckyHome.html

Kentucky Legislature's Web Site for Kids
lrc.ky.gov/kidspages/nav.htm